REVOLUTIONS
AND REVOLUTIONARIES

The Italian Problem in European Diplomacy 1847–49
Germany's First Bid for Colonies, 1884–85
The Course of German History
The Habsburg Monarchy, 1809–1918
From Napoleon to Stalin
Rumours of Wars
The Struggle for Mastery in Europe 1848–1918
(The Oxford History of Modern Europe)
Bismarck: The Man and the Statesman
Englishmen and Others
The Trouble Makers
The Origins of the Second World War
The First World War
Politics in Wartime
English History, 1914–1945
(The Oxford History of England)
From Sarajevo to Potsdam
Europe: Grandeur and Decline
(Penguin: Selected Essays)
War by Time-Table
Beaverbrook
The Second World War
Essays in English History
The Last of Old Europe
The War Lords
The Russian War, 1941–1945
How Wars Begin

REVOLUTIONS
AND
REVOLUTIONARIES

A. J. P. Taylor

ATHENEUM NEW YORK
1980

Copyright © 1978, 1980 by A. J. P. Taylor
All rights reserved
Design by Patrick Leeson
ISBN 0-689-11069-3
Typesetting and origination by Western Printing Services Ltd, Bristol
Printed in Great Britain by Ebenezer Baylis & Son Ltd,
The Trinity Press, Worcester, and London

First American Edition

Contents

Illustrations

6

Preface

This volume represents a return to my first love. As an undergraduate at Oxford in the nineteen twenties I studied the great French revolution and became even more fascinated by the revolutions of 1848, that turning point, in Trevelyan's phrase, (a phrase which I unwittingly stole from him in my *Course of German History*) when Europe failed to turn. When I went from Oxford to Vienna it was with the intention of studying the central European revolutions in 1848. Though I learnt a great deal about them and discussed them in many lectures, it is only now that I have got as far as writing a book about them.

In 1948, the centenary year, I had two inestimable experiences: one, to hear Namier's Waynflete lectures on the German Problem in 1848, lectures never published and indeed never written; the other, to attend the Congress on the Revolutions of 1848, organised by the French government to reaffirm the continuity of France's revolutionary tradition. In a less scholarly fashion, I have watched the Russian revolution as a contemporary, holding, I hope, a fair balance between impartiality on the one side and partiality on the other.

I have of course not attempted to cover all the European revolutions that have occurred between 1789 and the present time. My theme is the revolutionary tradition that began with the fall of the Bastille and ended, as far as Europe was concerned, with the establishment of the Soviet government in Russia, one might say from Jacobinism to Bolshevism. I ought to have said more about Italy, a country deeply affected by the revolutionary tradition, and also about Ireland, a country which had a revolutionary tradition all of its own. Somehow neither of these countries fitted into my pattern. I mention them as an act of atonement. The clear line of development passes them by. Otherwise I have tried to give a clear account.

The six essays were originally given as television lectures in 1978 and, as usual, I express my deep thanks to Eddie Mirzoeff, the producer, for giving me this most welcome opportunity. The lectures have now been given a more literary form. I have even corrected some of the mistakes.

London.   A. J. P. Taylor

1

FRANCE: THE FIRST MODERN REVOLUTION

Louis XVI, King of France, later known as Louis Capet

France: The First Modern Revolution

There have been violent political upheavals as long as there have been political communities: kings have been overthrown, empires have fallen, new dynasties have arisen. But only from the time of the great French Revolution have there been revolutions that sought not merely to change the rulers, but to transform the entire social and political system.

The French Revolution originated revolutions in the modern sense and it was not until after it that people knew what revolutions were like. Its events echoed down the corridors of history. There were to be new Reigns of Terror, new incarnations of Robespierre and many another Marat.

The French Revolution started quietly enough. For two hundred years France had been an autocracy or something near it. Louis XVI, although a soft gentle character, was in theory all powerful. He ruled France; in a sense, he was France. He was also in financial difficulties. The fiscal system was decayed and creaky. Louis XVI summoned the States General, the equivalent of our Parliament, to devise new ways of raising money. It had not met for nearly two hundred years, not since 1614. When it met again on 5 May 1789, Louis XVI was still ostensibly supreme.

Within a few weeks Louis XVI grew uneasy. He was afraid that the States General, already calling itself the National Assembly, would encroach on his powers. He decided to send it home. The National Assembly had not met in Paris. The old

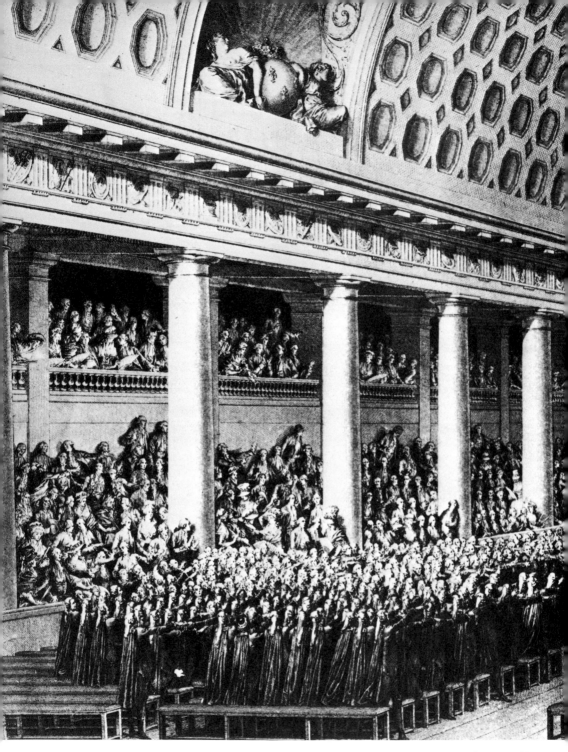

The States General becomes the National Assembly, 17 June 1789

18

19

The demolition of the Bastille marked the doom of the French monarchy

States General had always met wherever the king was and for more than a century past the kings of France had lived at Versailles. Paris, though by far the greatest city in France, was disregarded. The alarm spread in Paris that the National Assembly was to be dissolved. There was a spontaneous movement led by writers, journalists and orators. The symbol of royal power in Paris was the Bastille, a fortress of little real strength. It was garrisoned by a mere thirty soldiers, most of them elderly pensioners. The Bastille fell after a brief assault

20

and with it there fell also the French monarchy. On 14 July 1789 the French monarchy lost its historic prestige. Louis XVI was no longer King of France; he was merely King of the French, committed to a constitution. Historic France had gone and with it the prestige of the historic aristocracy. A new France had to be created. The National Assembly, summoned for a simple fiscal operation, now had to build a new social and political order.

The members of the National Assembly represented the

educated classes of France, a highly educated country. The French Revolution was not forced on the people merely by economic hardships, though the poor were indeed very poor. It was not even caused by practical problems. There was a long background of writers who called themselves 'philosophers', whom we should call intellectuals. They held an entirely new outlook on life: reason instead of tradition, a confidence in man instead of apprehension, above all a belief that the principles of society could be formulated in a few simple sentences and would endure for ever.

The French deputies of 1789 believed that they could make a clean sweep of the past. The monarchy was first defined by a constitution and then in 1792 overthrown. The aristocrats lost their privileges and sometimes their land, though many of them survived as wealthy landed proprietors. The Church also lost its lands and was put under the direction of the state. The traditional provinces—Normandy, Burgundy and so on—were abolished and replaced by new artificial *départements*.

The great achievement of the early French Revolution was the Declaration of the Rights of Man. Its very title was revolutionary. Not the rights of the king, not the rights of the upper classes, not historic rights. The Rights of Man were the rights of every citizen and rested on reason, not on tradition. The Rights of Man in their first formulation were modest: liberty, property, security and resistance to oppression. This last was included in order to sanction the revolutionary acts of resistance to Louis XVI who was in reality far from being an oppressor. 'Liberty' was the assertion that every citizen had the right to do what he pleased unless it was against the law.

'Property' was to become a cause of conflict later and in subsequent revolutions. In the past nobles had had the right to do what they liked in their castles, but the ordinary people in cottages could not. The Right of Property meant the right of every cottager to be free. Later people began to ask a different question about property: was it really satisfactory that a property-owner could do whatever he liked with his property even if this injured others? Could the factory-owner say, 'This is my factory and I propose to close it even though this will throw my employees out of work'? This conflict of rights was to shape much of modern history.

22

Louis XVI accepts the constitution, 14 September 1791

In 1791 the king accepted the constitution. It was formally declared that the revolution was over and that France had become a modern country based on rationalism and the Rights of Man. In practice the Rights of Man were a good deal restricted. Workers were denied the right to form trade unions. The right of the citizen to be represented depended on his property. Only the 'active citizens'—those with property—had a vote. The others were described as passive citizens, an inferior order. In theory universal suffrage was adopted for a few months in 1793, but no election during the French revolution was held on its basis.

From 1789 to 1791 there had been a logical pattern. The leaders of the revolution had clear ideas where they were going. Thereafter events took charge. The peaceful transformation of France into a constitutional country broke down. Louis had

23

The overthrow of the monarchy, 10 August 1792

25

Execution of Louis Capet, 21 January 1793

never sincerely acquiesced in it. He stirred up the reactionary powers of Europe to intervene in France and they welcomed the opportunity to weaken France or even to partition it.

War hung over France from the beginning of 1792. That summer it provoked the fall of the monarchy. On 10 August, the second vital date in the history of the revolution, Louis's palace, the Tuileries (to which he had moved in October 1789) was attacked. He took refuge with the Assembly and was formally dethroned. A month later the Republic was proclaimed. The French were confident that they were preparing a new age and that history would begin again from 19 September 1792, when the revolutionary Convention met. They dated years from that event: Year I, Year II and so on. Even the names of the months were changed into fancy words implying that it was a hot month or a cold month or a month with flowers. All were symbols that the new France was starting from scratch.

The more practical need was to face the challenge of invasion and this second Revolution was more the offspring of

The Republican Calendar

A revolutionary committee at work

panic than of novel ideas. In September 1792 there was a blind Terror, the massacre in the prisons, when priests, aristocrats and many others were killed. In January 1793 Louis XVI himself was executed. There was civil war in the Vendée. Many cities—Lyons, Toulon and others—broke away from the government in Paris, some to restore the monarchy, others to set up a federal system.

The revolutionary government that gradually emerged from the confusion and alarm still claimed to possess democratic principles and to speak for the people. In fact it was concerned

Jean-Jacques Rousseau, the philosopher of the revolution

to issue orders to the people. It was a revolutionary dictatorship. All the leaders of the French Revolution—like most leaders of most revolutions—came from the intellectual classes.
They were lawyers, journalists, professional men of one kind or
another. None were great aristocrats, none were peasants or
manual workers. All believed in enlightenment. All quoted
from the works of Jean-Jacques Rousseau. The division be-

tween the moderates and the extremists was one of temperament, not of class. The extremists or Jacobins as they came to be called were the 'hards', men who were prepared to sacrifice everything, including their democratic principles, in order to save France and the revolution. Such Jacobins existed throughout France. They were not a party in the modern sense: there was no formal party organisation. The Jacobins had their local clubs and they came together because they shared the same 'hard' outlook.

From May 1793 the Jacobins provided the revolutionary force and drive, embodied in the Committee of Public Safety, which represented the supreme dictatorship in Paris. They differed a good deal in character and policy. Marat, a journalist who had been at one time a doctor of medicine in Aberdeen of all places, was a man of violent phrases who demanded an open dictatorship and indeed called for the dictatorship of a revolutionary general. Danton, who had been a man of violence at the time of the massacre in the prisons, regarded violence as a temporary measure and was anxious to restore an easier life. Although he undoubtedly followed a patriotic line, he also made a modest fortune for himself. Danton did not share the idealism of the extreme Jacobins. When Robespierre spoke about revolutionary virtue, Danton replied, 'The only virtue I know is the one I practise every night with my wife'. Robespierre was shocked. Perhaps this was one of the reasons why he later arranged for Danton to be guillotined.

Robespierre I find difficult to admire. It is impossible to find real greatness in him, yet, because of his passionate faith in the principles of the revolution, he was perhaps its representative man. He was never more than the outstanding speaker of Jacobinism, not the creator of Jacobin policy. He was however the only politician ever known in any country to be called by everyone 'The Incorruptible'. Perhaps this quality was more surprising in France than in some other countries. Robespierre was incorruptible over money. He was corrupted by power. He had spoken against power. He had preached democracy. When he joined the Committee of Public Safety, he abandoned his principles. Though he still espoused the Rights of Man, he declared that these must be suspended until the peace. From June 1793 until July 1794 France had a revolutionary

Assassination of Marat, 13 July 1793

The rivals: ABOVE Georges Jacques Danton
OPPOSITE Maximilien Robespierre

government that stopped at nothing in order to conduct first a war of defence and then a war which would carry liberty across Europe. The Convention resolved 'to make Terror the order of the day'.

There was a *levée en masse* by which in theory everyone was conscripted into either the army or the munitions factories, while the aged were instructed to sit in the market places and encourage the recruits with patriotic songs. The French treasury had been almost bankrupt before the revolution. The

Warrant for the arrest of Danton and his friends

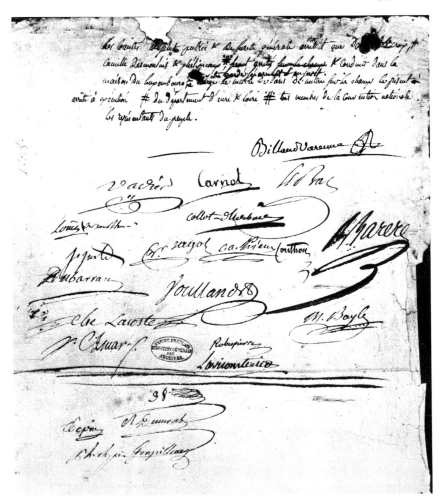

Paper money: an assignat for a thousand livres

mounting costs of the war made things worse. The Jacobins paid their way with paper money, that is, money they had not got. The result as we all know nowadays was inflation. The revolutionary government answered by the Law of the Maximum, freezing prices and to a lesser extent wages. The Maximum was enforced by Terror. Many of those brought before the Revolutionary Tribunal were there not as traitors or aristocrats, but simply for infringing the Law of the Maximum. There has never been a greater test of the idea that you can get rid of inflation by controlling prices and wages. The attempt failed. Inflation stormed ahead until years later when Bonaparte resolved that the French state should live within its income.

The sight of rich men making profits out of the war and the revolution led Robespierre and his close circle to a new view of virtue. The virtuous citizen was a patriot; he served in the armies; he observed the Law of the Maximum. The very fact of his poverty indicated that he was virtuous, thinking of France and the revolution, not of himself. If a citizen was rich, it was clear that he was interested in other things than his public duties. Robespierre and his disciple Saint-Just drew the moral. The poor were virtuous and should therefore be rewarded by a redistribution of property in their favour. Rich citizens were by definition less virtuous and should be regarded with suspicion, if not actually sent to the guillotine. This doctrine, like the French tricolour, was to make the circuit of the globe.

Robespierre and Saint-Just however had no time to apply their rule of virtue. Many members of the Convention had themselves made money during the war and they overthrew The Incorruptible in order to save their fortunes. In any case the need for revolutionary government was passing. By the summer of 1794 France was beginning to win the war. The national territory had been liberated. The natural frontiers as they were called had been reached. Between 1789 and 1794 France changed from a country with many different outlooks and even languages to a single nation. France had created nationalism. The nation could override tradition and history. Moreover France, as the Great Nation, could override the national claims of others.

Here were the three themes that revolutionary France launched into the world and that have continued to haunt the world ever since. They developed in many different ways. Nevertheless the three revolutionary causes—democracy, nationalism, socialism,—all sprang from the fall of the Bastille on 14 July 1789.

Robespierre's faithful follower, Saint-Just

2

CHARTISM: THE REVOLUTION THAT NEVER WAS

CAPTAIN SWING, THE RICK-BURNER

Evicted first from his farm to make room for a new fox-covert, and then
from his cottage for non-payment of tithe, "Swing" is explaining to the
clergyman on horseback the causes of rick-firing

Chartism: The Revolution That Never Was

In the later nineteenth century England enjoyed a unique reputation as the land of ordered freedom where the wisdom of the governing classes had so arranged things that no revolution was necessary and where the masses were content with the social system in which they lived. That was not how it looked at the time. There was a shortlived revolutionary movement which set an example to other countries and provided the model which others were expected to follow.

England was far from being orderly in the early nineteenth century. In the years after the battle of Waterloo she was indeed the most disturbed country in civilized Europe. In 1817 there was a large-scale hunger march: the march of the Blanketeers who proposed to take London by storm though they only got as far as Derby. In 1819 a vast demonstration in St Peter's Fields, Manchester, calling for parliamentary reform, provoked an onslaught by the yeomanry. Eleven peaceful demonstrators were killed, one of them my great-grandmother's cousin. Peterloo became a name to conjure with, a massacre that stood as a symbol of the old order.

In 1830, when the first Reform Bill was being discussed in parliament, there was the most formidable popular rising to take place in England in modern times: the revolt of the agricultural labourers. This revolt had nothing to do with the Reform Bill. It sprang from the poverty of the labourers and was directed against the threshing machines. The revolt was led by the legendary Captain Swing who perhaps never

The massacre at Peterloo, 16 August 1819

43

existed. He it was who sent messages of warning to those farmers or landed gentry who did not cooperate in the destruction of the threshing machines. Some time ago the BBC asked me to give a talk on the man I most admired in history. I offered to talk on Captain Swing. I did not receive a reply and never gave the talk. I take the opportunity to honour him now: Captain Swing, the eponymous popular hero, representative of the inarticulate masses who sought somehow to overthrow the hated system.

The agricultural labourers' revolt was repressed with great severity. Although only one man was killed in the whole course of the rising—and he a labourer shot dead by a member of the yeomanry, nine labourers were hanged at Winchester, four hundred were sent to prison and four hundred and fifty transported. The gentry of England, supposedly so kind and considerate towards their dependents, were by no means kind when there was a revolt by their own labourers.

The mid eighteen thirties produced a more coherent revolutionary movement. This did not break out suddenly as the great French revolution had done or as the minor French revolution of 1830 did. It developed from the activities of small political societies that had sprung up during the agitation during the passing of the first Reform Act. These little groups of educated working men—printers, artisans and writers in popular newspapers—voiced the radical interests and activities of the unenfranchised classes.

This radical movement was reinforced by the impact of the new Poor Law of 1834 which imposed harsh conditions on the unemployed. The impact was all the greater towards the end of the thirties when there was a period of bad trade. The agitation against the Poor Law turned particularly against the Bastilles, as the new workhouses were called. This agitation was greatest in the North of England. London, though the political capital, was not the capital of industry and had no great conglomeration of industrial workers. Cotton, the greatest industry of the time, was centred in Lancashire, wool in Yorkshire. The coal industry spread over Lancashire, Yorkshire and Durham; iron and steel developed in the Black Country round Birmingham. All were areas far from the political centre. In Scotland the great concentration of industry was around Glasgow—the only

44

Female ward in a workhouse

city in Great Britain where street barricades have been erected (1848) and also the only one where the Red Flag ever flew over the City Hall as a symbol of revolution (1919). The radicals went where the masses lived. The Chartist newspaper, *The Northern Star*, was published in Leeds and Manchester.

The People's Charter preceded the Chartist movement. It was drafted by members of the London Working Men's Association. The name of The Charter is significant. Radicals often follow historical precedents and they took the name in conscious imitation of Magna Carta. It was widely believed in

45

The Charter petition on its way to Parliament, 1842

those days that the people of England had been free until the Norman conquest which established the exclusive privileges of the aristocracy, duly enshrined in Magna Carta. The wealth and privileges of the upper classes rested on Magna Carta. If the People secured a similar Charter, this would make them as secure and prosperous as the upper classes were. There was also an imitation of the French Revolution. The Charter with its six points was an English equivalent of the Declaration of the Rights of Man.

The six points of the Charter summarised the traditional

The National Convention, 4 February 1839

Driving the Charter through Parliament

radical demands: adult manhood suffrage, equal electoral districts, annual Parliaments, vote by ballot, abolition of the property qualification for members of parliament, and payment of members—all except annual parliaments now achieved. It was not the detailed programme that mattered. The underlying belief of the People's Charter was that a democratic system of election would entirely transform the character of Parliament and society. Once the working classes, who composed the majority of the population, got the vote, all members of parliament would be working class and government would be conducted exclusively in the interest of the working class.

Most of the Chartists had great faith in what they called Moral Force. If the Charter were presented to parliament, together with a petition containing millions of signatures, the members would be overawed and would pass the Charter into law. The experiment was duly tried in 1839: the petition was rejected by a large majority. Again echoing the great

Feargus O'Connor, the orator of Chartism

John Frost, one time mayor of Newport, Monmouthshire, and Chartist rebel

revolution, the Chartists summoned a National Convention. The echo was somewhat muted: the English Convention comprised fifty three self-elected delegates, meeting in Bolt Court, off Fleet Street.

The Convention threatened a revolution unless the Charter were made law. Parliament did not cringe. The Convention then withdrew to Birmingham where they were nearer their constituents, the working-class masses. The Convention devised a programme of revolutionary action, framed in the form of questions. Would the workers strike for a month, the so-called 'sacred month'? Would they refuse to pay taxes? Would they abstain from alcoholic liquor and thus bankrupt the government? Answer came there none.

50

General Sir Charles Napier, friendly enemy of the Chartists

52

Charterville school building and cottages, recently demolished

The Convention never issued its call to action. There was not even a symbolic hour of idleness. There had been plans for an armed rising. These, too, were not implemented. Feargus O'Connor was the most dynamic of the Chartist leaders, a speaker who could hold a crowd of sixty thousand in the open air and much given to addressing them as 'Ye horny-handed sons of toil'. But though O'Connor's uncle had been a Napoleonic general, he himself was a man of violence in phrase only. Thanks to O'Connor there was no general armed rising, only one brave attempt in South Wales. In November 1839 John Frost, a Chartist who had been mayor of Newport, Monmouthshire, gathered a force of miners from the neighbouring valleys and attacked the Westgate Hotel in Newport, which was held by troops. The attack was defeated. Fourteen Chartists were shot. After the failure of the rising Frost and two other leaders were sentenced to death. Reprieved, they were transported to New South Wales, along with some two hundred other Chartists. The Westgate Hotel, scene of the last battle in English history, still stands, a little improved in Victorian times. I am also glad to report that there is now in the centre of Newport a John Frost Square, a delightful pedestrian precinct with a plaque to explain its name.

Frost's rebellion marked the end of the revolutionary movement. It had always been an unequal struggle. The armed

Victoria Station, Manchester. Railways helped to defeat the Chartists

53

forces were never affected by revolutionary propaganda. They were professionals who did their duty even though some of them may have been sympathetic to the Chartists. General Napier, who commanded in the North of England, was himself in favour of manhood suffrage. The new railways contributed decisively to the defeat of Chartism. With the railways Napier could base his troops in Manchester and yet move them to Birmingham or Leeds within a couple of hours. Similarly a detachment of metropolitan police were brought by train to Birmingham at the time of the Convention.

Though revolutionary enthusiasm flagged, the organisation of Chartism increased. There was a Charter Association with a subscription and membership cards. There were first rate writers, particularly George Julian Harney, from whom Marx got many of his ideas. It was Harney more than anyone else who defined Chartism as the political expression of the working class. There were still great meetings especially at times of industrial distress. But, since the members of parliament could be neither converted nor overawed, how was the Charter to be achieved? Even the most enthusiastic Chartists turned to more practical things: the agitator of yesterday became today secretary of the local cooperative store or trade-union branch.

Feargus O'Connor struck out on a new line. Being himself an Irish landowner, he recognised that many English workers wanted to escape from the factories and go back to the land. O'Connor set up the Chartist, later the National, Land Company. Enthusiasts bought bonds in the Company. O'Connor used the money to buy rural estates and on these estates built cottages—often literally with his own hands. When the cottages were finished, each with its two, three or four acres of land, there was a lottery among the bondholders and each winner acquired a cottage. The rents, it was assumed, would enable O'Connor to buy more land until the whole of England would be covered with Chartist smallholdings.

Alas, the smallholders rarely paid their rents. The National Land Company went bankrupt and O'Connor was ruined. He lost his reason and died in an asylum, a forgotten man. Yet the plan represented a deep desire of working-class people to keep in touch with the land—a desire that was to carry many of them across the seas to America and the British Dominions.

54

The Chartist settlements can still be seen, some of the most interesting, though not the best preserved, historical monuments in England. Heronsgate in Hertfordshire, known as O'Connorville, has kept its character best. Its narrow, rough lanes still bear the inappropriate names of Stockport Road, Halifax Road and Nottingham Road. Charterville near Oxford was also virtually intact until a couple of years ago when it was wantonly destroyed to make way for a housing estate. Now we must travel as far as Snigs End in Gloucestershire to see what a Chartist settlement was like at its full extent. The school, which was also the community centre, has become a public house.

Chartist school building at Snigs End

The Chartist Convention, John Street, Fitzroy Square, 1848

Chartism had a last splutter in 1848, provoked partly by the economic depression of 1847 and partly by the French revolution of 1848. Once more the Charter was brought out. Once more signatures were collected for a petition—five million it was said, though with much exaggeration. Once more a National Convention met, this time at John Street, Fitzroy Square.

On 10 April 1848 there was a great gathering on Kennington Common. The governing classes were much alarmed. In 1780 a similar gathering in St George's Fields, led by Lord George Gordon, had inaugurated the worst riots in British history. The bridges across the Thames were controlled by troops, with the venerable Duke of Wellington in command. Special constables, including Louis Napoleon and Charles Dickens, were enrolled. The precautions proved unnecessary. The Chartists brought their families and picnicked on the grass, now the Oval Cricket Ground. When Feargus O'Connor and other speakers were in full spate, Sir Henry Warren, the chief commissioner of police, arrived in a cab. He advised O'Connor to send the Chartists home peacefully. O'Connor agreed. The Chartists crossed the bridges in small family groups. There was no violence and no rioting. The Charter petition was taken to Parliament in a cab. I wonder whether it was the same cab as Warren had used. With this Chartism faded out of existence.

Many Chartists went to America in search of the free land and democratic life they could not find at home. George Julian Harney had a successful career there as a journalist. Many years later he came back to England, where he met leading socialists of the day, such as Hyndman and Bernard Shaw. He said of them, 'They are not such revolutionaries as we were'.

The demonstration on Kennington Common, 10 April 1848

3

1848:
THE YEAR OF SOCIAL
REVOLUTION

Louis Philippe, King of the French, abdicated 24 February 1848

1848: the Year of Social Revolution

1848 was pre-eminently the revolutionary year when almost the entire continent of Europe was swept by revolution. Russia escaped at one end of the continent, England at the other except for the Chartist demonstration. Virtually every other state in Europe experienced a revolution, political, social or both together.

Revolution in Paris on 24 February 1848 gave the signal for revolution to Europe. The revolutions were of two kinds. France had had her great revolution in 1789. Now she possessed a constitutional monarchy, two houses of parliament, a free press and a limited suffrage. East of the Rhine most countries were still ruled by absolute monarchs. There was serfdom, censorship and secret police. The Rights of Man were unknown. Thus one type of revolution sought to gain what the French had already—a middle-class liberal state; in France the revolution overthrew this middle-class state and sought to go beyond it.

The background to the revolutions was provided by the great Depression of 1847, the first time when mass unemployment ravaged the more advanced countries of Europe. Hundreds of thousands of men were out of work with no provision for the relief of themselves or their families. To some extent the revolutions began as largescale unemployed riots. There was also a more immediate cause: a demand by the parliamentary radicals for an extension of the franchise.

Proclamation of the Second Republic, 24 February 1848

The provisional government at the Hôtel de Ville

The method of agitation was characteristically French. The radicals held reform banquets where they made radical speeches; then they went home. The culmination of their campaign was to be a great banquet in Paris. It was forbidden by the police. The radicals wished to show that they were not afraid of the police and yet were law-abiding. They went to the hall where the banquet was to take place, read the order pinned to the door that it was forbidden and went home. Or rather they meant to go home. They were overwhelmed by mass demonstrations of the Paris workers. The following day, 23 February, these demonstrations increased.

Those who had previously supported the system backed away from it. The National Guard, a sort of armed special

Lamartine proclaims the republic

constabulary, who had put Louis Philippe on the throne in 1830, turned against him and he, anxious not to be responsible for a civil war, retired tactfully to England. The radicals in the Chamber of Deputies hastily botched up a provisional government. In order to proclaim it they went to the Hôtel de Ville, the traditional place for proclaiming provisional governments. There they found a rival group of rather more leftwing radicals who had already proclaimed a provisional government of their own choosing. Somehow the two governments were blended together. Such was the French revolution of 24 February 1848.

There was a brief period of euphoria. Lamartine the poet, himself a member of the provisional government, said, 'We are making together the most sublime of poems'. Baron de Rothschild, the richest banker in Paris, opened his house to the unemployed and served turtle soup and other delicacies to them. De Tocqueville relates how, when he returned to his apartment late one night, the caretaker said to him, 'Next week *you* will be answering the bell and *we* shall be dancing upstairs'. The practical symbol of emancipation was the introduction of universal suffrage—the first time in any great state and an innovation from which France never retreated.

After that the provisional government was stuck for a programme. Lamartine describes its members sitting round a table and debating the question what great thing they could do. After a long silence one of them suggested the abolition of capital punishment. That was all they could think of to justify their revolution. They abolished capital punishment. A few months later they restored it and applied it against the very revolutionaries who had carried them to power.

In the great French revolution there had been no separate category of revolutionaries. Robespierre with his powdered hair had not the slightest idea before the revolution that he would become a revolutionary conducting the Committee of Public Safety and the Terror. But from early in the nineteenth century there were professional revolutionaries. Though they did not make their living by this, it was their sole activity. If you had asked Blanqui or Barbès or Raspail what was his profession he would have answered, 'I am a revolutionary'.

Each revolutionary had his own group of followers and in

Auguste Blanqui, the persistent revolutionary

Barbès, Blanqui's rival

1848 his own club where he held forth. Some had elaborate
plans for the future society. Blanqui, the most significant and
powerful of them, was contemptuous of this. He took the view
that the revolution would provide the answer of itself. He said,
'I can make a revolution in forty-eight hours' and when asked
what would happen then, replied, 'If you are on one bank of a
river you can have no idea what are the problems on the other
side. *Let us cross the river and see*'. Blanqui always turned up when
there was a revolution, though usually a little late, because

Louis Blanc, the prophet of the social republic

whenever there was a revolution he was already in prison. In 1848 he missed the February revolution by a week because he had been in prison under Louis Philippe. In 1870 he missed the revolution because he was in prison under Napoleon III. He spent over forty years of his adult life in prison and only about four years in open political activity. For Blanqui the instrument of revolution was not democracy or universal suffrage. It was 'the dictatorship of the proletariat', a phrase which he did not define more closely. The other revolutionaries disliked

The national workshops at work

Blanqui as indeed they disliked each other. When Barbès was preparing the list for yet another provisional government and saw Blanqui's name on it, he said, 'Not over my living body' and struck it out.

Proudhon said of the revolutions of 1848 that they were made without an idea. Surprisingly one was found. It came from Louis Blanc, a radical journalist, who long before the revolution proposed in his book *The Organisation of Work*, the establishment of social workshops, workers' cooperatives we might say. Blanc asserted, as Robert Owen had done, that the workers' cooperatives would gradually supersede the entire capitalist system. Owen actually described his projected cooperative societies as 'the trains which are taking mankind to universal happiness'.

With the revolution of 1848, the Parisian workers who dominated the streets wanted some escape from unemployment and 'national workshops' were the answer. The provisional government and after it the National Assembly reluctantly acquiesced. From March until June something like a hundred thousand men or more received what was really relief on task work. The national workshops became a symbol of social justice to the working classes and were denounced the more bitterly by the individualist radicals. Thus the revolution moved from political to social emancipation.

Perhaps even more striking, Louis Blanc was put in charge of a commission, representing the various trades of Paris, to draw up a labour code, an early form of Soviet. This Luxembourg commission in its two months produced an amazing charter of working standards: limitation of hours, minimum wages and controlled conditions of work, the greatest advance made by the French working class until well on in the twentieth century.

Not a single member of the Luxembourg commission was an industrial worker. They were all skilled artisans. France was still in the pre-factory era. Though Blanqui called for the dictatorship of the proletariat, there was in fact no proletariat to provide the dictators. There was another class missing from the revolutionary forces of 1848. The great Revolution had been sustained throughout France by the rebellion of the peasants against the feudal system. Now that the peasants owned their land they were not interested in further revolutions. They

General Cavaignac, conqueror of the revolution

regarded with horror the talk about socialism which they thought meant the nationalisation of the land or, as it was called, 'the agrarian law'. The revolutions of 1848 were exclusively town revolutions and every town with more than fifty thousand inhabitants had one. The revolutionaries ignored the peasants, but with universal suffrage the peasants provided the majority of voters.

The revolutionaries of 1848 constantly attempted to push the provisional government into more extreme actions. They looked back to the great Revolution and re-enacted the same play. De Tocqueville, the historian who was a member of the old Chamber of Deputies and then of the National Assembly,

Parisian workers captured during the June days

describes how the mob broke into the Chamber. A revolutionary figure in the public galleries pointed his musket at the deputies and de Tocqueville wondered why he himself was not frightened. The thought suddenly came into his mind, 'That man's musket was loaded in 1793. He is not a fighting man. He is an actor repeating the gestures that he has seen in some picture of 1793'.

The men of 1848 were for ever re-enacting the scenes of 1793. The first great radical demonstration was strangely enough against holding elections. Blanqui explained that the people were not educated enough to vote (an argument usually of reactionaries); therefore the elections should be postponed until the radicals had time to educate them. When asked for how long the elections should be postponed, Blanqui answered, 'Perhaps for months, perhaps for years, perhaps for ever'. The extreme Left, once champions of democracy, had come to fear it.

At the second great demonstration on 15 May, the revolutionaries invaded the National Assembly and declared it dissolved. They spoke, they said, in the name of the people although they had not been elected by anyone. Of course it is very rare for a revolutionary ever to be elected. Marx was never elected to anything. Blanqui was never elected to anything. The distinguishing mark of a revolutionary is that he cannot get elected. With the provisional government dismissed, the handful of revolutionaries set up a new provisional government consisting of themselves. It lasted about a couple of hours. During this time just like their predecessors they debated what great thing to do.

They did not concern themselves with the National Workshops, a topic which did not interest the political revolutionaries. They resolved to restore the greatness of France as it had been in the days of the Jacobins. Their sole decree was an order that the rulers of Russia and Germany should at once liberate Poland. If they did not do so, France would go to war against them, a strange echo of 1792. Before any more decrees could be passed, gendarmes arrived and cleared the chamber. Blanqui and others were arrested. Many of the revolutionary leaders disappeared. The cause of free Poland was forgotten.

P. J. Proudhon: "universal suffrage is counter-revolution"

There followed a revolution without leaders. On 21 June the National Workshops were dissolved. Here was a clear repudiation of 'the social republic'. The artisans of Paris rose in spontaneous revolt. De Tocqueville describes a sinister scene. Walking down the boulevard in the early morning, he saw men systematically chopping down the trees to build barricades. There were no directors or organizers. Each man took his own initiative. With barricades erected in all the poorer districts, the provisional government resolved on civil war. More people were killed in Paris between 24 and 28 June than had been killed throughout the great revolution. De Tocqueville called it truly, 'The greatest slave war of modern times'—the lower classes on one side, bourgeoisie, the army and peasants hastening to Paris on the other. Something like fifteen thousand were killed during the June days, and many more afterwards. Twenty thousand were sent to prison or to the penal settlements overseas.

The events of the June days had left the political radicals ostensibly in power, though they were in fact dependent on the army and its commander General Cavaignac. The social revolution had been defeated, though the implication of the National Workshops that society had some obligation in regard to unemployment was to be of great significance in the future. The radicals still tried to apply their principles. In the abolition of slavery, the extension of education and the reorganisation of French institutions, they had an honourable record. This was not enough for them. Looking back to the Jacobins they wished to promote democracy abroad as well as at home and to enhance the international prestige of France.

During the great revolution the Jacobins had achieved national unity and had then set out to impose their revolutionary will on Europe. The radicals of 1848 aspired to do the same. But where should the work of liberation begin? The extremists, led by Blanqui, had pointed to Poland. The more moderate radicals preferred Italy which was nearer and which in the spring of 1848 had appeared to liberate herself. Then the radicals drew back. Was it really to the advantage of France that Italy should be united? They hesitated and did nothing. The great negative of 1848 was that the French armies did not intervene anywhere as liberators. Their only intervention was

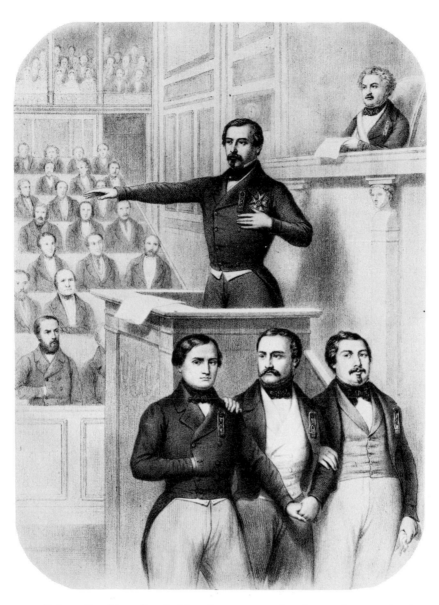

Prince President Louis Napoleon swears loyalty to the constitution

French troops assault the Roman republic, 1849

in 1849 when they overthrew the Roman republic and restored the Pope as absolute ruler of Rome. This was a foretaste of the time when once-revolutionary France became a conservative Power in Europe.

The end of the 1848 revolution was again a parody of the great French revolution. As Marx said, 'History repeats itself: the first time it is tragedy, the second time farce'. The great revolution ended with Napoleon as first consul and then as emperor. The second ended when Napoleon's nephew became president in December 1848, elected by that prized achievement of the revolution, universal suffrage.

Napoleon III was a feeble copy of his uncle. He was not a good general; he was not a good organizer. But although he was a dictator and an emperor, he was also something of a socialist. The revolutionary impulse of 1848 did not flag altogether. It was expressed by an absolute ruler who claimed to derive his power from the people. In fact, as Proudhon said, universal suffrage was counter-revolution.

4

1848:
THE YEAR OF
NATIONAL
REVOLUTIONS

Prince Metternich. His fall carried revolution into central Europe

1848: the Year of National Revolutions

The French revolution of 1848 was largely a repeat performance. The revolutions that engulfed central Europe were new, certainly emulating the French in some ways, but faced more sharply than the French had been with the problem of Power.

Just as the fall of the Bastille launched the great French revolution, so the central European revolutions of 1848 were launched by a fall, in this case the fall of a single man, Prince Metternich, Chancellor of Austria since 1821 and the symbol of reaction and repression. On 13 March 1848 discontented aristocrats persuaded the Emperor to dismiss Metternich, and with this the conservative order collapsed.

All the central European revolutions threatened the Austrian Empire. Austria dominated northern Italy, and the Italian revolutionaries aimed to expel the Austrian forces. Austria was the presiding power in the German confederation, standing in the way of unification. The Emperor was also King of Hungary and extended his sway over the lesser peoples of eastern Europe. Austria represented tradition. The new order sought to combine nationalism and liberal constitutions. The European revolutionaries of 1848 aspired to achieve the French constitution of 1791.

Sir Lewis Namier has called the revolutions of 1848 'the revolution of the intellectuals'. In a sense all revolutions are led by intellectuals except that peasant revolts are sometimes led by peasants. The leaders of the French and to a less extent of the Italian, revolutions were mainly journalists or, like Mazzini, writers of political books. The distinguishing feature of the German revolution was that its leaders were university professors, or at any rate academics, men who believed that by achieving a written constitution they would change the reality underlying it. The German revolution did not aim at the overthrow of monarchs. Indeed no German dynasty was dethroned by the revolution. One prince, the King of Bavaria, lost his throne but this was solely because he was having a love affair with a dancer, Lola Montez, and the Bavarians disapproved of this or rather of his spending so much money on her.

Written constitutions, for both Germany and the separate states, were the aim of the German revolution. Of course the French revolutionaries had attached great importance to the Rights of Man but they imposed these on Louis XVI by force. The reluctance of the German revolutionaries to use force revealed their essential conformity. They did not want any basic social change. They did not want power for themselves. They hoped that the monarchs would be peacefully converted to a mild liberalism, whereupon they in their turn would show loyal devotion to the August Houses.

Power was certainly a factor that the revolutionaries considered. Not power for themselves. Rather power which the monarchs would wield in order to maintain the academics in their property and social position. For academics, social position was treasured quite as highly as the possession of landed estates was by an aristocrat. The German revolutions of 1848 rested on a temporary alliance between the monarchs and the liberals.

In March 1848 the kings and princes were frightened. They granted constitutions but retained their thrones. Above all they retained their armies. In the great French revolution the army of the old regime was largely dissolved simply because the king of France could not afford to pay the soldiers. The armies of Prussia, of Austria and of the lesser states remained firmly disciplined forces, loyal to their king or emperor, not to the revolution. The liberals hoped to change this by an ingenious twist. The most prominent liberal demand of 1848 was that the German armies should take an oath of loyalty to the

A woman of mystery, perhaps Lola Montez for whom Ludwig I lost his throne

The revolution in Berlin, March 1848

The revolution in Vienna, 1 May 1848

constitution. Thus, the liberals felt, the revolution would be secure. Most of the soldiers were peasants, totally ignorant about the constitution or any other political idea. But once they had taken an oath of loyalty to the constitution, they would observe it. No revolutionary activity would be needed. There would be no struggle for power. There would be a peaceful transformation. The German Parliament at Frankfurt would devise a scheme for the unification of Germany and the monarchs would acquiesce in it, not because they were forced to do so, but solely out of goodness of heart. Above all it would not be necessary to call in the masses.

There was some social upheaval in the revolutions east of the Rhine as there had been in France. There were unemployed demonstrations and riots in Berlin and in Vienna. There was

Emperor Ferdinand, the Weak-Minded

St Paul's, Frankfurt, meeting place of the German National Assembly

Emperor Ferdinand flees from Vienna, 1848

even talk of National Workshops. Such talk alarmed the Frankfurt academics and placed them still more strongly on the side of the monarchs.

The peasants of central Europe also had their social discontents, particularly in Austria where they still lived under the restrictions of a decaying feudalism. The emancipation of the Austrian peasants was one of the few positive and lasting achievements of the revolution. It was carried through by the liberals of the Austrian parliament and endorsed by the Emperor on 7 September 1848 when feudal dues and services were abolished throughout the Austrian Empire. The peasants felt no gratitude towards the Austrian parliament. They believed that the emperor himself had liberated them as seventy years before Joseph II had attempted to do. From this moment the peasants became a conservative force, indifferent to parliaments or constitutions.

In Germany there was a central parliament at Frankfurt which claimed to represent the entire German people. There were however also parliaments in the separate state. There was a Prussian parliament in Berlin, composed of liberals more leftwing than those at Frankfurt. In November 1848, when the king of Prussia dissolved this parliament and repudiated the constitution it had devised, the liberals of Frankfurt were delighted. They thought that the victory of the king of Prussia over his liberals was a victory also for them. Similarly, when the Austrian army suppressed the liberal movement in Bohemia, the Frankfurt parliament sent a delegation to approve the acts of the Austrian army.

The achievement of a constitution was for the German liberals only a preliminary. Their overriding aim was to establish national unity. Nationalism was the great common factor in the central European revolutions of 1848. Indeed it was a spirit never to be exorcised thereafter. The great French revolution had inaugurated the idea of nationalism. When Louis XVI was overthrown, the French people took his place. But though the French people fought the Napoleonic wars in an inspired spirit of nationalism, this raised few territorial questions. The old French state already comprised most of the lands in which French people lived and could thus be transformed into the French nation without great extensions of territory.

The situation was very different east of the Rhine. A German sentiment had existed for a long time. An Italian sentiment had existed for a long time. An Italian state had never existed. Indeed Italy had not been united at any time in its history; even in the days of the Roman Empire Italy was divided into separate provinces. Germany had possessed the shadow of a state called first the Holy Roman Empire and in the early nineteenth century the German Confederation. But there was no clearly defined, united Germany.

Here was the great question of 1848: where was the German, the Italian or for that matter any other nation to be found?

The greatest prophet of radical nationalism was the Italian Mazzini. Mazzini believed that the creation of free nations

96

Mazzini, prophet of nationalism

would bring general peace throughout Europe: there would be no more national oppression and all would cooperate, inspired by a common ideal. But, as often happens with national enthusiasts, Mazzini also believed that the Italians would be the most inspired of all. Rome, once the capital of the Roman Empire and then the seat of the papacy, would become the leader of a new national Europe, a role Mazzini attempted to

Attack on the papal palace, Rome 1848

Field Marshal Radetzky, in his camp was Austria

play in the winter of 1848–49 when he was virtual dictator of the shortlived Roman Republic.

Territorially Mazzini had little difficulty. Like the French in 1792, he claimed that the frontiers of Italy had been given by God and nature. By a strange chance, natural and national frontiers happened to coincide. This was in fact not true. There were peoples not of Italian stock living south of the Alps: Germans in South Tirol and Slovenes, then an almost unknown nationality, in Istria. These anomalies were ignored. The natural frontiers became the aim of Italian national claims and were largely, though not entirely, achieved in the early twentieth century, despite protests from the non-Italian peoples concerned.

The frontiers of Germany presented a far greater problem first for the Germans themselves and then for other peoples. God and nature had not been active in regard to Germany: there were no natural frontiers. How then was national Germany to be defined? The German liberals found a simple answer. Just as national France claimed all the territories of the French monarchy, so national Germany claimed all the territories of the historic German states. This raised many problems, above all the problem of the Austrian Empire. That Empire was to outward appearance German. The Habsburg dynasty was German; the administration was carried on in German. Therefore the German nationalists asserted that the entire Austrian empire should be incorporated in the new national Germany. They were particularly emphatic in regard to Bohemia which had been part of the Holy Roman Empire and where in 1348 the first German university was established at Prague. When the Frankfurt parliament was summoned, instructions were sent to Bohemia for the election of members to the Frankfurt parliament.

In fact Bohemia was predominantly inhabited and had been for more than a thousand years by a people who were not German at all. They were Slavs, the Czechs. Czech Bohemia had lost its historic rights and been subordinated to German rule. By the nineteenth century however the Czechs were re-asserting their nationality. When Frantisek Palacky, a leading Czech historian, was invited to Frankfurt, he replied: 'I am not a German. I am a Bohemian of Czech nationality'. Palacky invented an idea which had a strong run in the later nineteenth century, though it subsequently proved barren. He regarded the Austrian Empire not as German but as a protection of the non-German peoples from the Germans and said, echoing Voltaire, 'If Austria had not existed, it would have been necessary to invent it'.

Bohemia was not the only problem for the Germans. Many Germans lived beyond the territory of the historic German states. To meet this difficulty, the German nationalists claimed that Germany existed wherever German was spoken. This did not mean that Germany existed where only German was spoken. In great areas of eastern Europe, the educated classes, the business classes and sometimes the landed classes spoke German, whereas the majority of the inhabitants, even in the towns and still more the peasants, spoke some other language—Czech, Polish or Croat. What should happen then? The German liberals gave a confident answer: these were lesser peoples and should disappear. This answer was given by Friedrich Engels, Marx's closest friend: 'The natural and inevitable fate of these dying nations was to allow the process of dissolution and absorption by their stronger neighbours to complete itself'.

The Germans made one exception. They agreed that the Hungarians were an historic nationality with their own historic institutions. The German liberals looked with favour on the idea of an independent Hungarian state. This was indeed the aim of the Hungarian revolutionaries in 1848: to establish a Hungary liberated from the Habsburgs either entirely or in all but name. Yet ironically the Hungarians or Magyars were themselves a minority in what they claimed as their national state. In the revolutionary year Hungary fought two wars: one against the Habsburg Empire and the other against the lesser peoples—Serbs, Croats and Romanians—who were seeking to liberate themselves from Magyar rule.

Early in 1849 Hungary won a shortlived independence. The Habsburgs were dethroned and Kossuth, the revolutionary leader, became Supreme Governor. Within a few months, the Habsburg armies, aided by the Russians, were victorious. Hungary lost its independence and Kossuth went into permanent exile, dying in Turin in 1894. But he always asserted his

Franz Joseph, Emperor of Austria, conqueror of the revolution

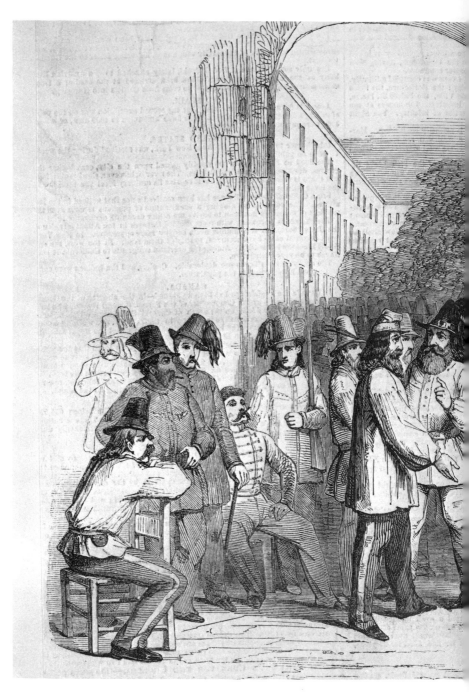

Garibaldi's headquarters, Rome 1849

title. At gatherings of exiled revolutionaries, Kossuth was announced as the Governor and the other revolutionaries were expected to stand up for the only one of them who had been, however briefly, a supreme ruler.

In the course of 1848 the German liberals came to appreciate that German predominance in central and eastern Europe could not be achieved by high principles but only by force—the right of the stronger. But what force? The liberals had no force of their own. The only force lay with the existing armies, particularly those of Austria and Prussia. The German liberals welcomed the reconquest of northern Italy by the Austrian army under Radetzky. Above all they determined to enlist the Prussian army in the national cause. This idea did not work out in 1848. The king of Prussia turned against the liberals and ultimately the Prussian army dispersed the Frankfurt parliament. In a longer perspective, the bargain was made. The German liberals acknowledged the overlordship of the king of Prussia. In return the Prussian armies united all the German states except for the lands of the Habsburg monarch. This was the work of Bismarck, the man who himself experienced the revolutions of 1848 and said of them: 'The great questions of our day will not be settled by resolutions and majority votes—that was the mistake of the men of 1848 and 1849—but by blood and iron'. After 1848 most German liberals would have agreed with him.

Yet the rise of a great united Germany was not the only ultimate outcome of the revolutions of 1848. In a longer perspective the awakening of the submerged peoples with no historic traditions who were now coming to life counted for more. Coming to life because of education, because of the railways, because of the advance of industry. More than anyone else the school teacher created nations. Illiterate people cannot be conscious what nationality they belong to. Once they become literate, there is no escaping national awareness. Take its most practical expression: the newspaper. When a Bohemian peasant could read, what newspaper should he buy—Czech or German? The answer determined his nationality.

In 1848 some of the non-historic nations already staked out their claims. Bohemia had for a short time its own parliament where Czech and German ranked at least as equal. The Serbs,

Lajos Kossuth, Hungarian leader and (briefly) supreme governor

Hungarians surrender to the Russians at Vilagos, August 1849

the Slovaks, the Croats, asserted their national claims. And something more. Slav peoples became conscious, perhaps exaggeratedly so, of belonging to a wider Slav community. That community did not exclude Russia. Tsarist Russia was a tyrannical country and the ally of every reactionary government. But it also had outstanding revolutionaries.

When in June 1848 a Slav congress met in Prague, there were not only representatives of the Czechs, the Slovaks, the Poles and the Serbs. There was also one Russian, Bakunin, later to be famous as an anarchist and an opponent of Karl Marx. What Bakunin represented in 1848 was the Pan-Slav idea that Russia would one day be transformed and would lead Eastern Europe towards national emancipation. Surprisingly however this emancipation was to come with the wars of the twentieth century.

5

REVOLUTIONARIES
WITHOUT
A REVOLUTION

Karl Marx, revolutionary student

Revolutionaries without a Revolution

The revolutions of 1848 had been expected to produce a large family of revolutions thereafter. In fact they marked the virtual end of revolutions for the rest of the nineteenth century. There were occasional disturbances such as the battle of Trafalgar Square in 1887. There was a revolution in Spain which overthrew the monarchy for a few years. There were rebellions in the Balkans, particularly the Bulgarian rising of 1876 which provoked from the Turks the Bulgarian Horrors. But revolutions such as there had been in 1848 faded away, leaving only an army of unemployed revolutionaries.

One episode is entitled to the name of revolution, though it was not intended to serve a revolutionary purpose. This was the Paris Commune of March 1871. The poorer classes in Paris had suffered greatly during its siege by the Germans. The French provisional government showed them little consideration. The Parisian workers refused to surrender their weapons, seized the Hôtel de Ville and set up a commune which put forward a few socialist measures. The Commune proclaimed the principles of socialist internationalism and destroyed the column in the Place Vendôme which commemorated Napoleon's victory.

The Commune was suppressed with great severity by the provisional government. Twenty thousand Parisian workers were killed and something like a hundred thousand deported. Karl Marx wrote a pamphlet glorifying the Commune and in

Meeting in Trafalgar Square, 8 February 1886

114

116

the twentieth century Lenin presented it as the model which the Soviets should follow. This did the Commune too much honour. It sprang from conditions at the end of the Franco-Prussian war rather than from deeper social causes.

The great French revolution had left a legacy of three revolutionary causes: democracy, nationalism and socialism. In the later nineteenth century the first two of these causes ceased to be revolutionary. Democracy was the first to become respectable. Universal suffrage, still a revolutionary cause in 1848, was introduced into Germany some twenty years later by Bismarck, a conservative. It was introduced into Austria in 1907. Even Russia had universal suffrage in 1905 for a short time. Curiously, it reached Great Britain almost last—only in 1918. The Reform Act of that year added more voters to the lists than all previous Reform Acts put together, but it passed almost without notice. Working-class voters rarely returned working-class members of parliament. Women voters, partly enfranchised in 1918 and fully ten years later, rarely returned women members of parliament.

Germany and Italy achieved national unification. Thereafter nationalism became a rightwing cause. The extreme nationalists were now reactionaries and opponents of democracy. Garibaldi's Red Shirts of the nineteenth century became Mussolini's Blackshirts in the twentieth. Revolutionary nationalism survived among the Christians of the Ottoman Empire. It survived to some extent in Poland. And of course it flourished in Ireland, a topic I have somewhat neglected. The Irish had a great national rising in 1798—The Year of Liberty—, an ineffective attempt at revolution in 1848 and Fenian outbreaks thereafter. In the early twentieth century the Irish peasants acquired their land and thereafter Ireland became a conservative country, despite a revolutionary war against the British from 1919 to 1921. And of course Ireland contributed radical leaders to Great Britain from Feargus O'Connor on.

Socialism was the only revolutionary cause left. Nearly all the remaining revolutionaries wanted some sort of basic social change. The revolutionaries received a reinforcement with the

Instructing special constables in their duties, Trafalgar Square 1887

A barricade, Paris Commune 1871

118

appearance of Russian revolutionaries, opponents of the tsar's absolutism, but also deeply concerned with social change. There was a gulf between the Russian revolutionaries and those from western Europe. Western Socialism was about industrialism and the proletariat, as the industrial working-class were called. The Russian Social Revolutionaries thought only of the peasants. They were concerned not only to emancipate the peasants but to establish a society built round the peasants. The social revolutionaries hardly recognized the industrial workers. Considering the backwardness of industry in Russia this was not surprising.

In western Europe the situation was quite different. Here industry and the industrial workers were the sole concern of the revolutionaries. For Marx and Engels the peasantry, just like the lesser nationalities of 1848, were doomed to disappear. Their place would be taken by large-scale capitalist farms as was already happening in the United States. In time these farms would be socialized and become the property of the nation. Marx often described the peasants as troglodytes—half-human beings living in caves. The idea that the peasants could become a revolutionary force did not occur to him until very late in his life when, looking at Russia, he vaguely imagined that there might be an alliance there between the peasants and the industrial workers. Russia was for Marx a special case, as indeed it proved. Otherwise in Marx's view only the industrial class counted as a revolutionary force.

The revolutionary exiles, most of them living in London, still thought of themselves as revolutionaries and talked in revolutionary terms. But they were no longer wild men. Engels was a jolly fellow who liked taking a party of revolutionaries into the country for the day and drinking lots of German wine. Marx used to run round his room with his little daughter on his back whipping him along. He also sent his children to private schools and provided them with expensive piano lessons. Despite the fact that no new revolution occured, the revolutionaries often had fun.

The revolutionaries without a revolution were reluctantly abandoning the idea that a new revolution would blow up over night. Blanqui was now outmoded. Characteristically he missed the Paris Commune, being—as mentioned earlier

Friedrich Engels, Marx's comrade

Murder of communards by the French army, 1871

122

Foundation of the First International, St Martin's Hall, London, 28 September 1864

—already in prison. Hence, while his followers were active in the Commune, Blanqui himself never had the opportunity to lead a revolution.

Marx and Engels took some time to change their outlook. After 1848 they still expected a new economic crisis which would provoke new revolutions. There was such a crisis in 1857 and Engels, by then a prosperous cotton merchant, wrote to Marx, 'There is a fresh depression and now the rotten system will collapse'. It did not collapse; it went on to prosper more than before. There was another depression in 1886, known as the Great Depression until eclipsed by that of 1929–33. But again capitalism did not collapse.

Hence the alternative came to be the building up of mass political parties, based on the working class. Marx and Engels

124

emphasized the class struggle as the key to history because they believed that, if they could win over the working class, they would at last command a large body of followers. With revolutionaries there was always a tendency to exaggerate the number of their followers. After all, if a revolutionary had no followers, there was not much point in his being a revolutionary. He would do better to become, as many exiles did, a business man, a musician or a writer.

Marx was expert at manufacturing armies of followers. In 1848, when he wrote The Communist Manifesto, he claimed to speak on behalf of communists everywhere and particularly on behalf of the Communist League in London, which he described as the voice of the international proletariat. In fact the Communist League in London had seven members, all

Meeting of the First International, 1866

126

German exiles and not one of them an industrial worker. One was a Prussian officer who had been cashiered for some offence; one was a rather dissolute cousin of Marx's. One was a printer, one a cobbler. Three other artisans made up the seven who together represented the international proletariat.

In 1864 Marx had become more ambitious and founded the International Working Men's Association, commonly called the First International. This caused a considerable stir in Europe. As late as 1873 the League of the Three Emperors—Russia, Germany and Austria—was created primarily to resist the conspiracies of the International Association which by that time was in fact dead.

The First International embraced almost every country in Europe and extended to the United States as well. Not every country sent delegates. This posed no problem: Engels or Marx himself took the vacant place. Engels regularly answered 'Present' when the secretary called 'Spain'. Marx for some time represented a district in New York, though he had never

Membership card of the First International

George Odgers, financial pillar of the First International

been to America and no one there had sent him any authority. As so often Marx simply appointed himself. The International was sustained by money from the English trade unions, the leaders of which, though not approving of revolutionary activities, were much impressed by 'the learned Dr Marx' and flattered to be told that the proletariat would one day be the ruling class.

This happy state of affairs was disrupted by the incursion of a rival revolutionary, Bakunin. Marx laid down that socialism would only be established by the dictatorship of the proletariat. In other words, government would become more powerful. Bakunin insisted that socialism would be established by the immediate destruction of all government. Once anarchy triumphed, the innate goodness of human nature would prevail and socialism would operate of itself.

Bakunin had the rare distinction for a revolutionary of actually being present at a revolution. This was at Dresden in 1849. He was present by accident. He had been staying with friends in Dresden and heard that there was a revolution in Prague. He set off for the railway station and found his way obstructed by barricades. To Bakunin's surprise the revolution was in Dresden, not in Prague. He mounted the barricades. Bakunin once started a revolution all on his own, at Bologna in 1875. He appeared in the town square with six or eight followers and announced that the Italian government was overthrown. No one took any notice.

Bakunin's closest friend in exile was a Russian officer who in fact was a Russian spy. The officer needed to justify his expenses in Geneva where he was operating with Bakunin and demanded evidence of imaginary conspiracies which Bakunin loyally provided. This evidence enabled the officer to claim an increase of expenses. When the officer was finally recalled, he and Bakunin had a sad leave taking at Geneva railway station, with the officer bearing letters to Bakunin's supposed followers in Russia.

Once in the International, Bakunin operated the same system as Marx and Engels had done. He fabricated branches, thus building up a large anarchist following among the watchmakers of the Jura. He also claimed large followings in Italy and Spain. Curiously enough the claim came true after

Michael Bakunin, Marx's rival

Bakunin's death, and until well into the twentieth century the Italian and Spanish anarchists outnumbered the socialists.

Marx and Engels were baffled by Bakunin's activities. The more they manufactured non-existent branches, the faster Bakunin outstripped them. The end came at the conference of 1872 when Marx in despair proposed that the centre of the International should be moved to New York, where he thought that it would be out of Bakunin's range. Sure enough it was. It was also out of Marx's range: the First International died.

Yet the First International left an unexpected legacy: the establishment of mass socialist parties, based on the working class. The German Social Democratic party was the most successful of these parties, becoming for a time the largest single party in Germany. Other socialist parties followed. Even the British Labour party, though not Marxist in theory, asserted in its very name Marx's doctrine that the emancipation

Allies in the Second International:
LEFT August Bebel ABOVE Jean Jaurès

OVERLEAF
The massacre outside the Winter Palace, 9 January 1905

of the working class must be the work of the working class itself.

The rise of mass parties challenged the traditional concept of revolution. What place was there for violent revolution in a system of universal suffrage? Engels laid down before his death in 1895 that the revolution would be achieved when the working-class party won a majority in parliament. Barricades and street fighting were, he said, obsolete as revolutionary methods, and the only people likely to resort to them would be reactionaries—a prophecy in which there was much truth. By the beginning of the twentieth century the German Social Democratic party, along with the other socialist parties of Europe, had become part of the established political system.

Most parts of Europe witnessed in the early years of the twentieth century a Utopia of liberty. There was freedom of speech, freedom of enterprise, freedom of movement, freedom of writing, on a scale which now seems to us fantastic and impossible. If we were offered the freedom which our grand-fathers enjoyed before the first world war we should not know what to do with it. We should be like men released after a long prison sentence, overwhelmed by our unaccustomed liberty.

This was not true in Russia. In Russia there was still absolute monarchy and there were still revolutionaries. Even the Marxists among them were divided. One group, the Mensheviks, argued that capitalism must come before socialism and that therefore the socialists must cooperate with the liberals to establish a middleclass constitutional state. The other group, the Bolsheviks, insisted that in Russia revolution must develop at once into socialism. Few people in the west took these theoretical arguments seriously.

I once asked Vandervelde, a Belgian socialist who had been chairman of the Second International before 1914, whether he remembered Lenin and Trotsky. He said, 'Oh, yes, I presided over the meetings of the International where they often spoke. Most delegates did not bother to stay and listen to them'. He added: 'I let them talk on. I knew they were not men of action'. This was the view of the Russian revolutionaries taken by the respectable, prosperous, successful socialists of the west.

In 1905 there was a surprising event—the first Russian revolution. As usual most of the revolutionaries missed its

136

On the way to Siberia, December 1905 (Trotsky marked with a cross)

outbreak. Lenin, the Bolshevik leader, got only as far as Finland and never reached Petersburg. Trotsky did better and in 1905 first achieved fame. The sensation of the revolution was the spontaneous appearance of hitherto unknown institutions, the Soviets.

The Russian revolution of 1905 was first diverted and then suppressed. The tsar recovered his powers, with the slight embarrassment of a tame Duma. Nearly everyone agreed that it was quite wrong to have a revolution in orderly civilized Europe.

Few pondered the question: was the Russian revolution of 1905 a belated echo of the revolutions of 1848 or did it presage a new era of revolutions?

6

RUSSIA, 1917:
THE LAST EUROPEAN
REVOLUTION

CHAPTER 6

Tsar Nicholas II and family celebrate the Romanov tercentenary, Moscow
1913

140

Russia, 1917: the last European Revolution

The Russian revolution of 1917 was the unmistakable progeny of the great French revolution and its nineteenth-century successors. Those who experienced this last revolution often called on the great names of the past. Trotsky emulated Danton; the opponents of Lenin accused him of following Blanqui instead of Karl Marx; and the Council of People's Commissars saw themselves as a new Committee of Public Safety. Some two months after the Bolshevik seizure of power, Lenin wrote to Trotsky, 'This is a moment of triumph. We have lasted a day longer than the Paris Commune'.

Most of the earlier revolutions had started unexpectedly. The Russian revolution of 1917 was no exception. In January 1917 Lenin, then in exile in Switzerland, told a group of Swiss students, 'Revolution in Europe is inevitable. We of the older generation will not live to see it, but you youngsters will see it'. Lenin was wrong on both counts: he lived to see the Russian revolution but the Swiss youngsters never saw a revolution in Switzerland.

Again like most of the previous revolutions, the Russian revolution, though it had profound causes, broke out more or less accidentally. In the nineteenth century Russia had produced an incomparable body of revolutionaries, ranging from social democrats to anarchists and nihilists. A tsar, Alexander II, had been assassinated. A prime minister had been assassinated; a grand duke had been assassinated. There had been an

"End the war", Petrograd, May 1917

unsuccessful revolution in 1905. Nevertheless Russia entered the war of 1914 with a burst of patriotic enthusiasm. A few Bolsheviks were sent to Siberia, but most social democrats and all liberals supported the war, just as they did in Germany and in the Entente countries. The discontent which gradually developed was not created by hostility to the war, but by dissatisfaction with the way it was being run. As in France before 1789 with regard to Louis XVI, there grew up a belief that the failures of government—the incompetence, the mili-

142

tary defeats and the lack of food in the towns were due to the tsar personally, a view shared by some members of the imperial house and by most of the generals. A similar belief led in England to the overthrow of Asquith by Lloyd George and to the establishment of Clemenceau as prime minister of France.

The actual outbreak of revolution took everyone, including the revolutionaries, by surprise. It began as food riots, an echo of 1848. Although Russia was a great food-producing country, the call-up of the peasants, which was almost universal, together with the strain on the railways to keep the armies supplied, led to food shortages in the towns. There was inflation and a flagrant contrast between rich and poor. The demonstrations of February 1917 were simply a protest against the bad conditions, particularly in Petrograd, the capital.

The original revolution was entirely a Petrograd affair. It is often suggested that the revolution was due to military defeat and discontent at the front. This is not so. The Russian army of 1917 was a better fighting force than it had been at the outbreak of war. Indeed one recent authority goes so far as to say that the Russian army was as well equipped in March 1917 as the French and British armies were in the summer of 1918, when they were able to achieve decisive and final victory.

In Petrograd the original demonstrators were joined by soldiers from the garrison—elderly men whose only wish was not to be sent to the front. There was a cry for the overthrow of the tsar and he was easily persuaded to abdicate. From that moment, as Trotsky said, 'Power fell into the street'. There was not even a constituent assembly, only an antiquated duma, which somehow fudged up a provisional government, composed of liberals and a few social democrats. The man who personified the provisional government was Kerensky, a revolutionary orator whose main anxiety was to arrest the revolution and even to reverse it. Kerensky was the Lamartine of 1917.

There was however a rival authority which echoed the Paris Commune of 1871: the Soviets first established in Petrograd and soon in every town in Russia. The Soviets were the equivalents of trade councils. There were delegates from the factories, from the army and, with some pretence, from the peasants. The Soviets were not concerned to govern. They wished only to enforce their practical demands on the provisional government. There was thus a balance of power or more correctly a balance of impotence. The provisional government had little authority. The Soviets shrank from exercising the authority which perhaps they possessed.

Moreover the Soviets had few leaders. When they sought to set up an executive committee, they put on it anyone whose name they recognized and these happened to be mainly moderate socialists who happened to be in Petrograd. Most of the

Alexander Kerensky, provisional head of the provisional government, 1917

Bolsheviks were in exile. Stalin was in Siberia. Lenin was in Zurich. Trotsky was a film extra in New York. Virtually the only Bolshevik left in Petrograd at the beginning of the revolution was Molotov, a university student who had escaped exile solely because he was unimportant.

It was only some six weeks afterwards that the Bolshevik leaders returned to Russia. They led a very small party. It claimed twenty-five thousand members, but many of these had lapsed, were in prison or had gone to the front. The Bolshevik, soon to be called the Communist, party seemed more formidable mainly in its leaders than in its followers. They were by no means clear where they were to lead. Some of them always wanted a further revolution. Some shared the Menshevik heresy that there must be first a period of liberal capitalism.

Joseph Stalin from police records

Stalin in better circumstances

The overthrow of the tsar and the establishment of a provisional government did not produce a miraculous improvement overnight. Quite the contrary: when the traditional autocracy fell, nothing took its place. There was no genuinely elected parliament which might have represented Russia. In this strange Russia of 1917 the only way to represent Russia was to claim you were doing so. On what grounds did Kerensky for instance represent Russia or democracy? He had not been elected by any one. He had few followers and an inflated reputation. He had appointed himself spokesman of the provisional government and was warmly applauded in western countries as the democratic leader because he proclaimed Russia's determination to continue in the war.

In much the same way, Lenin had never been elected to anything. Trotsky had at least served on the Petrograd Soviet of 1905. Lenin, to the best of my knowledge, was not even elected to the advisory board of readers at the Zurich public library where he had spent most of the war. Lenin rose to power simply by his own insistence that he could rule. This insistence was by no means accepted at first. When Lenin first proposed to the executive of the Bolshevik party that they should seize power, the other members were so shocked that they agreed to destroy every copy of Lenin's resolution. (One survived by chance). Lenin merely laughed and said, 'The people of Russia are a hundred times more revolutionary than we are'.

The great difference between the second or Bolshevik revolution and all previous revolutions was the presence of Lenin: a man of supreme determination which he could impose on others. He was a heavy Germanic speaker, not a great orator like Trotsky. He imposed himself on his followers and then on great masses of the Russian people by the force of his personality. Confident in himself, he captured the adherence of others and became a legendary figure during his own lifetime.

Lenin claimed to be the most orthodox of Marxists and indeed in September 1917, just before the Bolshevik revolution, wrote a book to prove it: *The State and Revolution*, firmly based on sacred texts from Marx and Engels. Unconsciously perhaps, he also echoed other revolutionaries. Like Blanqui he was confident that he could make a revolution in forty-eight

148

Trotsky and Lenin, 1917

hours. The only difference between Lenin and Blanqui was that Lenin succeeded.

Lenin took over the dictatorship of the proletariat and interpreted it in much the same way as Marx had done. The proletariat voiced its opinions through the Communist Party. Therefore the dictatorship of the proletariat meant the dictatorship of the Communist Party. The Communist Party in its turn voiced its opinions through Lenin. Therefore the dictatorship of the Communist Party was the dictatorship, sometimes a little obstructed by others, of Lenin.

Lenin had no doubt about his own ability to rule. When the first All-Russian Soviet met in June, one speaker said there was no single party which was prepared to take over the running of Russia. Lenin called out, 'There is such a party'. Few at that time believed him.

Russia remained in a revolutionary state throughout the summer of 1917. Or rather not so much a state of revolution as of increasing disintegration and confusion. The old order had largely broken down. No new authority took its place. The provisional government was little more than a symbol of impotence. The army, which had still been an effective fighting force before the revolution, began to break up under the impact of the revolution with its vision of a new Russia. In July 1917, when Kerensky tried to restore the prestige of the provisional government by an offensive against the Germans, this led to military defeat. This marked the end of the old army with the soldiers simply going home.

In July there were more food riots. Inflation grew worse. There seemed no prospect of recovery except the old dream that some powerful general would restore order. There was no such general. By now the generals shared the discredit which had overwhelmed the tsar.

The Russian people were increasingly anxious to get out of the war. This was Lenin's strongest appeal. The provisional government, which claimed to be democratic, sought to show its devotion to democracy by remaining faithful to Russia's allies who were supposed to be fighting for a more democratic world.

Lenin had a rigid conviction that if the Bolsheviks seized power and proclaimed that the war was over, this would have an immediate effect all over Europe. The German soldiers would lay down their arms; the British and French would follow suit. Thus peace and international revolution would be achieved at the same time.

Lenin was far more concerned to end what he called the imperialist war than to establish a Bolshevik dictatorship solely in Russia. He was after all an international Marxist who had spent most of his life abroad and thought always in European terms. Indeed he came near the Menshevik view that Russia was too backward to establish socialism all on its own.

Lenin in youth, 1897

Lenin in maturity

153

A second Russian revolution was to be merely the spark which would fire the mine of international revolution. Once that had been achieved, the centre of revolution would move westwards and Russia would be sustained by the more advanced socialist countries until she, too, built up her industrial strength. Lenin said as much himself. When the Third or Communist International was founded in 1919 and met in Moscow, Lenin said, 'We have to start somewhere'. He added, 'I am confident our next meeting will be in Berlin'—that is, after the successful German revolution. Faith in an international revolution was both the inspiration and the undoing of the Bolshevik revolution.

For there was a Bolshevik revolution on 7 November 1917. This was not a revolution of the masses, as the first revolution of 1917. It was the seizure of power by a small group on the model of what Blanqui had attempted in 1848. Yet, though the Bolsheviks had talked often enough of seizing power, in the event they, too, were taken by surprise. It was Kerensky who gave the signal for the Bolshevik revolution by determining to take the offensive against them. The Bolsheviks resisted under the leadership of Trotsky. To their bewilderment Kerensky and his government collapsed.

By 7 November 1917 the provisional government had dwindled to a meeting of ministers in the Winter Palace. Contrary to the dramatic scenes in Eisenstein's famous film, the provisional government was not overthrown by a mass attack on the Winter Palace. A few Red Guards climbed in through the servants' entrance, found the provisional government in session and arrested the ministers in the name of the people. That was the Bolshevik revolution. Six people, five of them Red Guards, were casualties of bad shooting by their own comrades.

There was a second seizure of power. The second meeting of the All-Russian Soviet was in session. It was told that all power was now in the hands of the Soviets. A few minutes later Lenin appeared on the platform and read out the names of People's Commissars—the new Soviet government. The People's Commissars had not been nominated by the Soviet and most of those present had little idea who they were.

Lenin announced two revolutionary decrees. The first was

Russian troops in revolution

the decree on peace which envisaged an immediate end to the
war and a peace based on the principle, 'no annexations and no
indemnities'. This was the spark that was to start the international revolution. The second was the decree on land. The
Bolsheviks had no land policy of their own. They certainly had
not advocated giving the land to the peasants. But this is what

Trotsky arrives at Brest-Litovsk

Lenin alone in convalescence, 1922. Stalin's ghost was added to the photograph some years later

Lenin now did. An indignant social revolutionary called out, 'That is our programme which you have opposed for years and now you have stolen it'.

The decree on land was supreme opportunism, designed to win the support of the peasants. It largely succeeded. In the ensuing civil war and the wars of intervention the Russian peasants, despite their dislike of socialism, preferred the Bolsheviks, who had given them the land, to the reactionaries who they knew would take it away and restore it to the aristocratic landowners.

Bolshevik Russia survived. Lenin's greater expectations were not fulfilled. International revolution did not sweep across Europe. At the end of the war in November 1918, there were revolutions of a sort in the defeated countries. There were no fundamental changes. In Germany the kaiser was dethroned and, after some alarms, a democratic republic followed with extremely moderate social democrats in charge. There was certainly no social revolution. There was a short-lived Communist revolution in Hungary, but its main

First Congress of the Third International, Moscow 1919

concern—another echo of 1848—was to preserve the territory of historic Hungary.

By 1920 the revolutionary impulse in Europe had died away. There were changes in the map of Europe. There were new states. But capitalism emerged relatively unshaken. Lenin had counted on international revolution. How was Communist Russia to survive in a world of capitalist states? Trotsky answered—by permanent revolution, seeking to provoke further revolutions elsewhere. Lenin agreed that socialism in a single country was impossible. His answer was simply that they must wait, much as the revolutionaries who had failed in 1848 waited for the new revolution which they expected in 1857.

The Bolsheviks, too, had become revolutionaries without a revolution. With Lenin dead and Trotsky in exile, Stalin determined to operate socialism in a single country after all. This was certainly revolution of a sort, though hardly one that the old revolutionaries would have recognized. Thanks to Stalin, Russia became a world Power. After the second world war, she imposed on some of her lesser neighbours a system of government by communist satellites.

In Europe, though not in other parts of the world, the old revolutionary inspiration flagged and died when the socialist revolution failed to become international after the Bolshevik seizure of power in 1917.

160

Lenin and Krupskaya. Domestic close to a revolutionary life

Index

163

164